The Late Wisconsin Spring

PRINCETON SERIES OF CONTEMPORARY POETS

The Late Wisconsin Spring

By John Koethe

Princeton University Press, Princeton, New Jersey

Copyright © 1984 by Princeton University Press
Published by Princeton University Press, 41 William Street,
Princeton, New Jersey 08540
In the United Kingdom: Princeton University Press,
Guildford, Surrey

All Rights Reserved
Library of Congress Cataloging in Publication Data will be
found on the last printed page of this book

ISBN 0-691-06620-5-cloth
0-691-01414-0-paper

Publication of this book has been aided by a grant from the
Paul Mellon Fund of Princeton University Press

This book has been composed in Linotron Janson

Clothbound editions of Princeton University Press books
are printed on acid-free paper, and binding materials are
chosen for strength and durability. Paperbacks, although
satisfactory for personal collections, are not usually
suitable for library rebinding

Printed in the United States of America by
Princeton University Press, Princeton, New Jersey

for Robert Dash

Some of these poems have been published in the
following magazines:

Broadway: "A Long Lesson"

Brooklyn Review: "In the Park"

Cream City Review: "Another Kind of Love," "The Little Boy," "The
Narrow Way," "A Sunny Day"

Epoch: "The Substitute for Time"

Grand Street: "Dark Bedroom," "Each One as She May"

New York Arts Journal: "The Near Future"

Paris Review: "The Guarded Optimist," "Malignant Calm," "One
Light," "Picture of Little Letters," "A Refrain"

Poetry: "Kinderszenen," "Partial Clearance"

Poetry in Motion: "The End of the Summer," "The Room Next to the
Mind"

ZZZZ: "Objects in Autumn"

"A Long Lesson" was also published as a pamphlet by Bouwerie
Editions (New York, 1974). An earlier version of "The Narrow
Way" was published in *United Artists*.

Contents

I

The Guarded Optimist

I can't tell you much about it yet.
I can offer only these general impressions
Of captivity, of the self as a creation of captivity,
A creation of delayed speech. They're less messages
Than the products of a desire to be there with you again
Talking with you, and being apart with you again that way.
It isn't a feeling so much of being alone
As of having been here too long, locked in a trance
Of expectation after the other, awkward shapes had moved
    away.

What were they? I thought I saw the reflection of my face
In the window, but it was merely some of those objects I have
    become now,
Shrouded in a haze of personality like a perfume.
And if we could lose that, maybe it would return the sense
Of what all of this was like, with the blood roaring in the ears
Like the drone of something that used to live here
A long time ago, before you and I came to be.

Dorothy Wordsworth

All my life
I've meant something I don't really know how to say—
Roughly, that *now* and *then* and *here* and *there*
Are different times and places, but not different ways of doing
     things;
And that every time and place is so dense
It can't hold any of the others,
But only sits next to them.
It's as though the "knowledge of experience"
Were that experience didn't matter all that much,
And that what I thought and meant and wanted
Didn't make very much difference, and that the past was a
     demonstration
Of how little weight the soul actually has.

And yet I still like most of the things
I used to like in high school, and I still think
Some of those wonderful, vague things *are* me.
I guess the things one has always liked
Don't have much to do with what one is, was, or ultimately
     becomes—
But I feel lost without them.
Fixed on something so far away my whole
Life seems prolonged out of proportion to the real world,
Things float in and stop and try to talk to me
And I agree with everything they say, though their voices
     aren't mine anymore:
It's getting awfully late. And we've all
Been up for a long time. In just a little while
All of us are going to be sound asleep.

Sometimes I can almost visualize my life
As a succession of those states—
Feelings of finitude, inklings of infinity
And the occasional breath of a human detail—
And it terrifies me to think that those moments could comprise
    everything I was ever actually going to feel.
But Dorothy Wordsworth went about her chores
In the throes of a dependency "so greatly loved
And so desperately clung to that it couldn't risk anything
But a description of the scenery in which it was lived";
And somehow accomplished her imagination.
And the long walks her brother took
In a phase of mind at one remove from description
Seem almost tangible now, and as funny and real
As the minutiae of real life.
Only they seem "absolutely small."

Puffy-lidded, doe-eyed,
With the detachment that characterizes
The fanatic, to whom nights and days are like children's stories
That don't explain anything but, taken together,
Make a fundamental kind of sense,
The sense of the mirror—
I thought I'd composed my life
Around a series of weightless moments,
And that each moment culminated in one of those remarks
People made at home, or overheard,
Or lost track of in a conversation,
And which were supposed to be as light as feathers.
But now I don't think anything like that ever really transpired
    at all.

Each One as She May

One life is enough. One private story
Lived out on a summer day. The play of the wind
And the fastidious vacuity of the mind
Lifting the chaos of emotion at the heart of life

Into these clouds of feeling, these reflections
Of the glancing voice upon the dark, unformulated sob.
The birds are singing and the mind is still.
This is how my life was always going to be.

But another time it might have quietly opened out
To take in all of the vulgar disarray
Sprawled out here under the uncomprehending sun.
A simplifying memory might have smiled and sighed

Because it knew its kind of happiness could never end
And that a moment of eternal recompense and peace
Lay in the cool sweetness of the summer shade.
But now the days go by and each one is the same

For life is reading and respite from reading,
And living in a vague idea of where the others are,
Or in dreams, or in these simple versions of the past.
So let the wind die and the birds fall silent

And the gladness of the summer afternoon dissolve
Into these light, distracted semblances of life
Drawn from a purely private story of unwritten grief
And happiness, for myself and strangers.

A Long Lesson

I spent a summer growing in that dream.
I looked—each day a little differently—
At what was there, and put it down:
The child, the family, the pets,
The ones who really tried to pray to God,
And the others, who only stared at him
In disbelief, excused themselves, and left.
I slammed the kitchen door and went outside.
It was a nice day. The flowers waved at me.
The little leaves vibrated in the breeze.
I lay down on the lawn and went to sleep
But it was always the same dream: the house
Was full of strangers; they were calling me
To come inside, but finally were still.
It was quiet and the backyard started
Glowing like a magic garden, cold
And green and full of trees, and when I tried
To wake I only grew, until I woke up looking
Into someone else's eyes at what I was:
What I would always be, but blind.

Let him sleep. And let the others
Heal in their hate: I hid my heart.
The child bore me down without a word.
His art was gentle, his emotions were
As vague as hills, and his spirit stank,
But the pockets in the air he breathed between
Were my whole life. He gave me everything;
He forgave; he took the world away.

If I was a wall about myself, still
I knew I lived in heaven: quiet rooms
Full of pleasant furniture and lots of plants
And all day full of sunshine; and at night
The light of tiny steel stars. Only
There was another world—it was a wonderland
Of happiness and ruined homes, that even God
Could only look upon in suffering.
But it was mine. I tried to live in it.
I felt it sob inside me like a child.
Sometimes I thought I heard him calling me;
Sometimes I knew that I was only crying,
That he *was* the other life we shared
Before we grew: our little sacrament,
My tomb, my throne, my poor God's body
Broken on his world, a world he made and
Opened to the boy in innocence. And later,
When he became a man, I knew I was alone.

O let him know the hurt, the happiness
That separates the hunger and the fall,
O bring him home! But he never healed.
He was my home. He was the altar where
I worshipped what I was, and made it die:
The garden where he slept; the dingy room
Where he was practicing the piano;
His school uniform; the funny little shoes
He wore in paradise; his attitudes; his eyes
That stared me back across the sweet decay.
It wasn't that he was unhappy or
Unsatisfied or too satisfied or mean—
But that he never went away. He led me
Deeper in his dreams, until I thought
That I could live alone with what I knew:

That far beyond myself I was a boy;
And that he was all of heaven that I had.

Where is that world, the one I made
From prayers for its return, the world where God
Is slowly dying for us through eternity?
Even to see it is to see it fade.
How could we stand the slow love, or
Endure the solitude that might have freed us,
Or the certainty that should have made us
Happy to be free? Where all day long
We wandered back and forth below the huge trees
And when night came and the summer moon
Was motionless, stirred in our dreams, as though
Even the slightest motion would have made them real.
Could we ever bear to be so happy? But it died
And died in us so differently it almost
Seems I might have never needed you:
I might have never looked at you
Through eyes the same as yours, through tears.
Or was that happiness? I could have dreamed
All those other lives. Wasn't it enough to dream?

He might have lifted me through the leaves,
Over the houses where the hate was sleeping,
Through the sunlight; and I might have seen,
Immaculate with snow, the floating mountains
Limiting the world, a world so beautiful.
Poor seed—poor blind seed shed from heaven,
Swollen in the earth until it grew—
Our lives change. And our worlds, like dreams
So absolute even our sorrow seems
A form of happiness, are being changed.

9

Objects in Autumn

"Either objects have life
And active power, as we have;
Or they are moved and changed
By something having life and active power;
Or they move and change us."
—The verbs are still in the mind
And the mind is still in the scenery
After thirty-seven years.
We must have seen what we came to see
And said everything we wanted to say
A long time ago: the terse
Survey and the faces of the angels
Reflected in it, which are like ours.
It's as though you and I had become
Caveats, slogans of speculation
In a world which is its own motto:
The bright colors of the trees
And the mild brilliance of the mind
In autumn, and the year-long helplessness.
Each thing speaks for itself
But with so much room around every word
And so sleeplessly, that the soul fails
And is left at the mercy of a few things.
Or is this waiting? Your quiet face
Crossed by glances, and my own mind
Stuck with secrets, indulging dreams
In which all its secrets explode?
But we have to swallow our dreams, for
As Thomas Reid observed, "A lively dream
Is no nearer to reality than a faint one,"
And the feelings of one or two people

Are theirs, are real, and can be contained.
Maybe we could have been as happy as
We are now, safe in that middle knowledge
Things have, and with complete lives
Lived out in detail, like the remote consequences
Of all that we'd ever wanted to say to each other.
But we never lived that way.
And now when I try to look at us
I can see only the settings, the distinct
Stages we inhabited just a little while ago
And this room where we started talking.
Eventually, our lives had to come true;
And the figures on the other side of the lens
(The figures in the living room)
Had to keep acting the same way,
Repeating the patient, perfect life
Ad interim, in a quiet room next to the mind.
We never left there, did we?
You and I are still at home, meaning to leave
In a little while, and meanwhile
Drawing the same dream closer
And closer around us, like a shawl.
But the days and the nights
Don't cut anymore; and the confusion,
The repair, the little things I did
And what I talked to you about, are all held
In words like boxes, gentle worlds
Whose inhabitants aren't even human;
And the window over your right shoulder
Gives on a verbless worlds of things
We meant to live through, a landscape.

Kinderszenen

Like that bird there, it alights and sings a song
And flys away again. And I don't want it to stay—
It's too early and I'm not quite ready for them yet:
I'm still thinking about them. And I know that the only true
    way is patience,
But if I could remember their names, remember what the trees
    looked like,
Or the details of that afternoon . . .
But a soft summer rain fell last night, and this morning the
    breeze was back.
It must have happened sometime during the night
Or early this morning while I was still sleeping,
And at first I didn't notice that anything had changed.
For I spend so much of my time alone,
Watching myself for the first, faint stirrings of a life
Which isn't mine anymore, and which I know can't be
    apprehended that way,
That sometimes the moments seem to lapse entirely inside me
On a transparent screen, or in a world where nothing real is
    ever going to happen.
Only this afternoon everything seemed changed: my friends
    weren't there,
But somehow it didn't bother me that nothing was ever going
    to bring them back again.
I kept listening to the wind: its purling sounded like time
Repeating something I'd been listening to for years, but hadn't
    had the character to say:
That they weren't real. That they'd only inhabited my
    imagination
Because it was empty. And that I didn't care what happened to
    them anymore.

For as I thought about them this afternoon
They began to seem weightless, and the oppressiveness of
    nearly twenty years
Seemed to fall away, leaving me alone in a small room
Trying to write a poem whose figures were unreal
Shadows cast by a single moment on the rest of time,
On the remainder of the world. After all, what were they
But the mirroring surface of a sob as it flooded a mind
Crammed full of useless details, like the traffic noises
Carried here on the wind, or something I said years ago,
One summer afternoon, to some friends whose names I can't
    even remember anymore.
It doesn't matter who they were. They kept me alive,
Protected from the others by a child's picture of what the
    world was like
Before they disappeared, like whole moments, back into time.

Partial Clearance

Barely a week later
I'd returned to myself again.
But where a light perspective of particulars
Used to range under an accommodating blue sky
There were only numb mind tones, thoughts clenched like
　　little fists,
And syllables struggling to release their sense to my
　　imagination.
I tried to get out of myself
But it was like emerging into a maze:
The buildings across the street still looked the same,
But they seemed foreshortened,
Dense, and much closer than I'd ever realized,
As though I'd only seen them previously in a dream.
Why is it supposed to be so important to see things as they
　　actually are?
The sense of life, of what life is *like*—isn't that
What we're always trying so desperately to say?
And whether we live in between them,
Mirror each other out of thin air, or exist only as reflections
Of everything that isn't ours, we all sense it,
And we want it to last forever.

II

The Little Boy

I want to stay here a while, now that there came to me
This other version of what passes in my life for time.
The little boy is in his sandbox. Mom and Dad
Are puttering around in the backyard.
"I stopped it once because it made me nervous,
But now look at what the waiting has done to me:
Particulars passing in and out of my mind like notes of rain,
The waiting for the clouds to go away. I think that there's
A secret behind all this, and moments like the moment
Held in his eyes as they floated up through the surface of the
    water,
When one by one the feelings fall away, leaving only a lacy
Network of lightning cracks in the black china sky."

I don't want the little boy to die.
I think there's something in the air behind that row of trees
But whenever I look there's just sky, sky behind more sky,
And the moments unfold in it. I move around a little,
Rearrange some things, make a few minor adjustments,
And then night comes. Then I know what it was like today.
But what changes means much more than what comes later,
In the quiet hour after dinner, or in these quiet little
Waystations on the road to silence.

Picture of Little Letters

I think I like this room.
The curtains and the furniture aren't the same
Of course, but the light comes in the window as it used to
Late in the morning, after the others had gone to work.
You can even shave in it. On the dresser with the mirror
Are a couple of the pictures we took one afternoon
Last May, walking down the alley in the late sunlight.
I remember now how we held hands for fifteen minutes

Afterwards. The words meander through the mirror
But I don't want them now, I don't want these abbreviations.
What I want in poetry is a kind of abstract photography
Of the nerves, but what I like in photography
Is the poetry of literal pictures of the neighborhood.

The late afternoon sunlight is slanting through the window
Again, sketching the room in vague gestures of discontent
That roll off the mind, and then only seem to disappear.
What am I going to do now? And how am I going to sleep
    tonight?

A peculiar name flickers in the mirror, and then disappears.

Malignant Calm

These things left in your hands,
Part calculation, part the unguarded effects
Of casual introspection, hormonal swings,
The close weather we've been having lately,
Aren't less human for what they hide, for what they
Mean without, somehow, ever quite managing to say—
Only weird, and sometimes just a little bit hard to absorb.
The eye glances through them and moves along, restlessly
Like sunlight bouncing from wave to tiny wave,
Working the surface into an overall impression
Of serenity and mature reflection, a loose portrait
Of the face of early middle age. They are not meant
For anyone, yet reveal, like the tight corners of the mouth,
An intensity that overwhelms the things I wanted to say to
    you,
Blurring whatever it was that brought us together like this
    again,
Face to deflected face, shouting into the other as though it
    were a cave
And I drew my life from the echo of what I told you, from
    what you said to me.
Sometimes they even seem like enough, sufficient unto the
    day.

A Refrain

Because we thought we had to know everything
About each other, only did already
Without realizing it, a sense of false
Expectation and foreboding, abstract and natural,
Began to alter the very look and sound and feel
Of what we said and did, earlier each day
Until now nothing but what confirms something
Someone knew or suspected all along is left for us,
And we stay where we are, in this place we have lived
For so many years, looking out the window at the water
And the city skyline in the distance. That is the refrain
Of a song that runs throughout the summer,
Of the girl sleeping in the sun and the face reflected in the bus
    window,
The song of the neighborhood children,
Seeming like something that hasn't really started yet,
To be grasped and understood later, only to come alive
A little too late, after the others, the serious
Incautious ones, have given up or lost interest,
Weary of it all, and decided to go back home.
What kind of urge is it, anyway? Wanting simultaneously
To accept and penetrate these surfaces that exhaust the human
    mind
Thirty-odd years later, but sickened and dismayed
By their indifference to everything we want them to be,
It returns us to ourselves as to the face in the cradle
Where the lullaby started that was to detain us for
The rest of our lives, constant through surface changes,
It intensity varying as the world moves up or farther away
Or recedes to the verge of death. It is what keeps it alive and
    waiting
For our own ends, meaning just as much as we meant it.

A Sunny Day

So this is the fruition
Of all our intense reflection about
The mechanisms of our lives: same kind of day,
Same smooth buds about to burst into bloom,
Same old junk on the lawn. Easy things these,
And maybe omens also of a kind of life that is best for us,
The most realistic kind of life for you and me.

Yet a while ago it was supposed to be different today,
With the sucked-out vacuum refilled by a vigorous new
Sense of attention to the small things around us,
Things meaning little or nothing in themselves, but which in
       chorus
Promised to spurt out a song of the whole world,
But whose relation to each one of them was to be transparent.

Working patiently and productively
This emotional farm yields, by the end of summer,
Merely a stack of artful impressions of a lapse of memory
Concerning the big things in our lives (whatever they were),
With the juice squeezed out, and the veins full of a thin fluid
Of the wrong kind of dreams, the kind we didn't know about
Until it was too late to do anything, after they had come true.
But this must have been what we were meant for

All along, and mistook for a poor and disappointing thing
In the half-light of a fantasy of living inside each moment
As it came over us for the first time, early in the morning
Just as the fog was turning bright and starting to lift.
We have lived here, in a dispositional sense, most of our
       lives—

Basically at home, occasionally out galavanting around
   somewhere—
Only now this thing we belong to is free finally
To admit us in our undisguised form, sweeping us along
In its stagnant motion, around and around.

Another Kind of Love

What is this we know so much about
But can't talk about, and don't want to hear about either?
Maybe an abstracted silence filling up the time in
A petulant refrain for two voices—only we've heard that
Long enough now, and now it is time to start over.
There's a fuller key, mixing the cool sunlight and the green
Trees with the cozy sound of the cold wind at night
Near the end of summer, relaxing the past
As it's really still part of us, soberer now and more tangible
But more genuinely alive. And there is room in it for love,
The spectacular kind that tears you open forever
But also—and this is the important thing—the kind of
Love for inconsequential things that aren't little only once
As they snap into cold focus through a lense of tears
And then just as suddenly evaporate back into the past.
That is a kind of love too, more a breeze than a vision,
Springing from an acceptance of the things we can't have
And a compassion for what we can't see anymore
But which brings them all back to us, leaving us all alone
On the border between two colors, green and gold.

The End of the Summer

A few more words spun out into a song
About the sense of singing, and then it is time
To put them away, to come back to them again later.
Summer drizzles away. Only this kind of singing
Leaves us with a quiet like a kind of love
In the corners of a story of our own blindness
To one another, alone and alive. And between it
And the fuller semblances to come, a period of life
More simplified and solid, of inattention and waiting—
Until the waiting starts to feel like happiness again
And the gaze wanders off without direction
Towards the autumn sky and the muted
Reds and yellows of the autumn leaves.

The Room Next to the Mind

The people I met today
And the ones I dreamed about last night
Are harder to find now.
Maybe it's time I stopped watching.

Under the true sky, in a room
The little mind can't hold anymore,
The muslin curtains bulge in the breeze
And it's nearly light.

I don't know what to do anymore.
Like an idle, endless sentence
Meant to mention everything,
Each day starts in company

And misdescribes,
Its frugal mess holding only vague
Prospects of peace and quiet when it's all over;
And then bed again.

What have I done?
Half mind, half music,
And people held so long under music
They're like monsters now,

Smiling, not even happy.
On Wednesday they start to cry
But it's just a spell: Sunday they're out on the lawn
And the waltz is humming, under the trees.

I thought about "home" today.
The people were standing there, scratching their heads
And wondering what had happened . . .
Whatever happened to them? Small and old,

Dwindling into view
Less and less frequently; and then never?
Diminished World, why don't your promises ever
Balance your remains?

I know my life has been
The weakness of a wish, all chorus,
Without too much pain or happiness.
But now that part is over.

III

The Narrow Way

When I was finally struck by
The infinite variety of human
Aspiration and greed, the multiplicity
Of forms of resentment, the generosity of kinds of kindness
And of instincts for disliking one another,
I had become used to thinking of the mind as
Nothing, in itself, but the unstructured story
Of an implied reader, an unobserved sequence
Of grainy images unrolling to the tune of a popular song
Rhythmical in intent
And musical in the memory
Of having once been still, that in the course of time out of
    mind
Might come to seem to smile again
And change, cry out a little and then die
As history, and its discarded argument start to come to life
    again.
For there isn't the urgency there used to be
About the individual soul, that elaborate,
Sometimes beautiful secretion of
A common sense of memory, holding in its hollow
Enough of the past for its purposes,
Our shared purposes, but genuine enough despite that;
There isn't the impulse there once was
For the expression of its kind of character:
What someone meant, or meant to mean,
The sifting of that casual mixture of intuition and debris
That animated words now issued stillborn from the lips
To float across a page of pure paper that no longer represents,
But rather seems to be, their very soul.

Where is the harm?
There used to be this vague idea of God
Lurking below the surface of our lives, but it is all words now.
And the lamentations of the lost, the poorly used, the slowly
    dying
That used to play about the minarets of heaven
Have become a kind of discourse on the lateness of the hour, a
    constant
Wistfulness masquerading as a form of play
On absence, the absence of the imaginary
Words it used to be our simple happiness to say.
But it is still early.
I was wondering the other day
How poetry still manages to move people
(Since any illusions about its ability to do so
Should by now have been definitively dispelled),
And my first thought was that it might somehow be due to
That experience of the movement of experience into memory
That is the breath of time, the static motion of the soul
On the border between sight and silence,
Flux and the mind—or in so many words
The feel of dying without the catch of death
To validate it at the end, seductive and mild
As a wind without the temperament to daze, to fill the eyes,
Refreshing but replacing nothing,
The style of change without the
Verifying annihilation.
But still, where is the harm?

The clear notes of decay,
Like glassy chimes, transsumed
The sentimental music of a slow accordion
Floating over the water late one night
In Paris, late last July.

Orange and blue lights
And the liquid melody of bells
Moved in my memory as another day began.
I felt again that reflex of dissatisfaction
Twitch in my mind, explode,
And then suddenly become still.
And now it seems like years and years ago
I started, out of a perverse curiosity,
This imaginary conversation on the border between my self
And the unimaginable pith or emptiness within.
And it proceeded for a while
Only to dissipate at the point of telling
Like a morning dream, or like the morning vapor off the water.
For these are vagrant promptings
Nothing stays, that nothing really acknowledges as its own.
But somehow they manage to continue in their own way.

And now no one can see me
And, in a funny kind of sense, I feel free.
But my feelings take so long to recognize themselves
That all at once it is late in the afternoon again
And once more it is time for me to be back at home.
And I've ranged farther in this conversation
Than ever before, but where am I? Sun,
Smile down on me. And breeze,
Elevate me into recognition.
For I want to stay outside.
The poetry of displacement,
The poetry of reconciliation the sudden sunlight dissipates—
Maybe those had only seemed to go away. The sense of
A sense of introspection plays about me
Here inside my wilderness night and day and
Night and day throughout my memory,
Pulling me to sleep

And waking up beside me every morning
Cloaked in its odor, which is the faint and fading atmosphere
    of dreams.

Don't you remember how real the music seemed
The first time, and how evasive it has now become?
Invading the interstices
Of a soul that is the sum of its impressions
It corrodes the sense that kept it whole
Until we fell apart, all mixed up in each other.
And now I watch you in your dressing room
With the one-way mirror as you watch yourself
Preparing for the punishment of being seen.
Because we both grew up in isolation,
Even an imaginary one, and didn't so much
Crumble in the air as dissipate a little
Like clouds, it gets harder every day
To separate the moments from the memories
Of what we did with them, or what we are
From what you were and what I wanted to become.
For these are memories as well
That echo in the way we talk to one another
Of what we have now, what there is
And what there always was, which should have been enough
    for both of us.
Somehow there always seems to be so little.
Time is without us and is unimaginable
But as a history of regrets, a severing of
Your intermittent voice from one that cries incessantly
And is the same thing as myself, the silent story
Time has to absorb before the real kind of history can start,
Start to forget us.
But I still love the way it sounded

Twenty years ago, the summer that became
The way we picture time, the bright disguise
Death wore the first time, before you and I had really learned
    to see.
But now the time has come for both of us to know.

I live here in a meaningless mythology
Of disappointment and the harbingers of change
And yet I can't even imagine life without you.
History sustains us from the outside,
Living all around us and without us
By its neuter laws of artifice
And annihilation, domination and defeat
That have no place for us, and yet confine us.
The deep chords of our being are outside history,
In disappointment and change,
Disappointment and the possibility of change,
And then finally only disappointment.
Why should we end there?
The inanity of desire,
The sanity of empty space,
The thought of heaven, the presentiment of hell—
These things are really signs of the indifference of the soul
To what is all around it, which it cannot see.
Why should we end there with it?
There are moments pregnant with a past
Still to be born, a future that doesn't know us
But is still our own, this very present issued from an
    inspiration
Lost to us now, but by which we manage to exist.
Sometimes I think that history is nothing but a way of talking
About a single moment, of pronouncing the present
So that it seems like the outcome of the sequence of the styles

That used to move us, that used to speak to us
While we could still hear, and now can only speak to one
    another.
And what in this am I?
The accidental focus of a name
Blending a million disparate moments into an arbitrary chord
Of happiness, that then dissolves?
But there are only atoms in the white
Refrain inside each individual soul, and only
Pain and tenderness to stay the emptiness of time,
Only mortality.

Stay with me out of tenderness awhile.
Soon time will cover us, scatter what we say,
Empty even these feelings that suffuse
The way I hold you now, the way you look at me.
Time is what makes these separate moments ours
To hide in, to give each other,
Or to give away; the rest are just invented
Fragments of a future we can never hope to see.
And as though I'd lived them all before
And now could see you only in my own reflection,
Each moment is a dying,
A severing of something that was here and now has left us,
Which both of us have given up our very lives to be.
The soul is what eludes us.
But all this was a way of reaching
Through myself into the empty space
We are to one another, hidden in a sense
Of what is absent from the world
Time comprehends, which holds
Something we are and cannot know we are
But as what passes.

IV

The Late Wisconsin Spring

Snow melts into the earth and a gentle breeze
Loosens the damp gumwrappers, the stale leaves
Left over from autumn and the dead brown grass.
The sky shakes itself out. And the invisible birds
Winter put away somewhere return, the air relaxes,
People start to circulate again in twos and threes.
The dominant feelings are the blue sky, and the year.
—Memories of other seasons and the billowing wind;
The light gradually altering from difficult to clear
As a page melts and a photograph develops in the backyard.
When some men came to tear down the garage across the way
The light was still clear, but the salt intoxication
Was already dissipating into the atmosphere of constant day
April brings, between the isolation and the flowers.
Now the clouds are lighter, the branches are frosted green,
And suddenly the season that had seemed so tentative before
Becomes immediate, so clear the heart breaks and the vibrant
Air is laced with crystal wires leading back from hell.
Only the distraction, and the exaggerated sense of care
Here at the heart of spring—all year long these feelings
Alternately wither and bloom, while a dense abstraction
Hides them. But now the mental dance of solitude resumes,
And life seems smaller, placed against the background
Of this story with the empty, moral quality of an expansive
Gesture made up out of trees and clouds and air.

The loneliness comes and goes, but the blue holds,
Permeating the early leaves that flutter in the sunlight
As the air dances up and down the street. Some kids yell.
A white dog rolls over on the grass and barks once. And
Although the incidents vary and the principal figures change,

Once established, the essential tone and character of a season
Stay inwardly the same day after day, like a person's.
The clouds are frantic. Shadows sweep across the lawn
And up the side of the house. A dappled sky, a mild blue
Water color light that floats the tense particulars away
As the distraction starts. Spring here is at first so wary,
And then so spare that even the birds act like strangers,
Trying out the strange air with a hesitant chirp or two,
And then subsiding. But the season intensifies by degrees,
Imperceptibly, while the colors deepen out of memory,
The flowers bloom and the thick leaves gleam in the sunlight
Of another city, in a past which has almost faded into heaven.
And even though memory always gives back so much more of
What was there than the mind initially thought it could hold,
Where will the separation and the ache between the isolated
Moments go when summer comes and turns this all into a
    garden?
Spring here is too subdued: the air is clear with anticipation,
But its real strength lies in the quiet tension of isolation
And living patiently, without atonement or regret,
In the eternity of the plain moments, the nest of care
—Until suddenly, all alone, the mind is lifted upward into
Light and air and the nothingness of the sky,
Held there in that vacant, circumstantial blue until,
In the vehemence of a landscape where the colors all disappear,
The quiet absolution of the spirit quickens into fact,
And then, into death. But the wind is cool.
The buds are starting to open on the trees.
Somewhere up in the sky an airplane drones.

The Near Future

I used to think that the soul
Grew by remembering, that by retaining
The character of all the times and places it had lived
And working backwards, year by year,
It reached the center of a landscape
Time couldn't penetrate, a green and white house
Surrounded by a chorus of trees,
Whose rooms were always filled with other people.
And now I think that it was just scenery,

The private illusion of a world
In which the "I" is the mind of an object,
And lacks features, and is part of the world in which it has to
    try to live.
For the soul knows that it's empty
And longs to dissolve, like a stray dream,
Back into nature, back into those things
Which had never seemed quite clear enough before.
But until now it could only see itself.

I used to think that there was a wall
You could touch with your hand, but not understand,
And that the soul had to pass through it alone.
I thought that other people's lives
Were like the walls of a room, keeping me inside,
Away from those things that were my real nature—
The houses, trees, and curbstones,
The noisy birds outside my bedroom window
And the thick ticking outside—
Taking the time that real things require.

Why do real things have to take so long?
I knew that time needed things, but there were so many
And they exploded like birds when I was almost close enough
    to touch them,
And then drifted back into the near future,
The center of the year.
But the furniture isn't as dense as it was
A few months ago, and it's finally quiet outside,
And there are a couple of empty rooms upstairs.

The Echo Chamber

As I lay me down to sleep
In this spiral lullaby, the solid
Wrap of thought that had clung about my days
Dissolved and I started falling, falling
Through my eyes into a solitary
Dream of telling, in my imagination,
The stations of the soul: of its creation
In the recognition of the startled face
That became its own; and its sense of time,
Which is the memory of that face become
A moving image of eternity.

It is a darkness permeated by
The memory of love, an abstract womb
Of night in which the smaller memories
Loosen and dissolve, and the dissolving soul
Cries out to them and slowly disappears.
It is a longing after nothing, fixed
Between the mirror of nativity
And the deep mirror of its own reflection;
Caught in an echo, in the bright mirage
Love pulled from nothing into light and air,
Into the possibility of happiness.

For the soul is an illusion of a soul
Held in an image of the endless space
That is its true home, but beyond recall.
It lives in time and is absorbed by time
But the happiness it longs for is its past.
Its impulse is the secret life it saw
In the reflecting eyes of a small child,

A life reverberating with the low
Echo of love, the echo of lost time,
Time that is over. But the small pleasures
That came to seem like happiness remain.

It woke up in a dark bedroom, the same
Dark room that I woke up in as a child,
But it isn't the same. It's as though
Each moment were another aspect of
The same timeless soul, and time itself
Merely the echo of its own creation,
An old incident in the darkness.
But even as it fades into the night
That once gave it substance, a wide happiness
Still surrounds it like the air, sustaining it
Inside the lengthening shell of that first sudden cry.

Dark Bedroom

O where did the light winds go
That used to stir the air about the summer trees?
The stars are coming out against the pale sky
And the evening air is motionless.

This is a sphere of thought and talk and dreams
I live in, where the summer night falls lightly,
And the intact memories of home float up and die
As an imaginary calm settles over the mind

And is unreal. The nightlight in my room
Intensifies the darkness while the isolating wind
Sighs in the corridor outside the bedroom door.
I am six years old again, and then I'm alone

And a beautiful moon fills the sky with transparent light.
Where is that happiness I knew so many years ago?
Or was it only casual fears held in the passing
Solitude of recollection, here under the summer stars?

One Light

Later we began to learn to live
At the mouth of this well of the pure desire
For an end of wanting, the descent into the sun.
The days unfurled like flags across the sky
Of cerulean blue, but the dreams were blank,
The evenings vague and apprehensive.
One by one the small songs twinkled away
Until only the sky music occupied our minds
With its stunned lament, and the brown eyes
Lowered finally and started to fill with tears.
We had been thrown into the middle of a landscape
Of an earlier imagination, an older dispensation
Swarming with wraiths and threats of immortality
Delivered in plainsong, with a grim air of purpose
Surrounding each detail of our preparations to depart.
It was the country we grew up in,
The scene of our nostalgias, where the warm
Twilight penetrated to the bone and the soft sea
Swept up towards an ambiguous horizon.
Then we moved into a world of towers and trees
Burnished by the autumn sunlight, grey stone paths
That emerged from the floating snow of winter
And spring rioting everywhere, that seemed
Torn from that book of dreams we kept rereading
In the aftermath of fear and disappointment.
The words leapt from the page into the mind
And vanished there, lost in the translation
Of forgotten things into the objects of a wish,
But meanwhile the formal part went on: the candles lit,
The folded napkins stiff with possibility.
And finally the distracted singing started

That grew up gradually into another life
Behind the strange one in the mirror, casting back
Into an imaginary past for what the others knew
Only to throw away, and thrusting us in ignorance
Into this endless now of restlessness and speculation
With the sky sealed tight, the tired mind withdrawn
Into a fable of itself and all the magic afternoons
Reduced to a single image of golden sunlight
Wavering over the soft grass. We have gotten older,
And the cave we started out from has become our home.

*   *   *

I know that today is everything
And change is an illusion fostered by
The loss of what we are, of our collective past.
The myth of how we came here, each one following
The course of some peculiar purpose written in the sky
Or held in the static frieze of time—I know that
That self-dramatization is delusion, empty cant
Hiding the shapeless breath that sings for nothing
But the singing itself, the mortal breath that cries into
The echo of the half-remembered cry that is its own.
But that is what time feels like from inside
Where the story of our common life unfolds in a darkness
That is taken from it at the end, torn into fragments
And blown like bright clouds of confetti across the sky.
It is the culmination of the dark dream of progress
That begins in wanting and finishes in a quiet conversation
Held at the mouth of a grave, our grave, that trembles now at
    the approach
Of the blazing void that widens as we fall out of the darkness
Into a deep field of light, back into endlessness.

The Substitute for Time

*How things bind and blend
themselves together*

Ruskin, *Praeterita*

I came back at last to my own house.
Gradually the clear, uninhabited breath
That had sprung up where the spent soul disappeared
Curved in around me, and then it too slowly disappeared.
And I have been living here ever since,
In the scope of my single mind, the confines of a heart
Which is without confinement, in a final pause
Before the threshold of the future and the warm,
Inexhaustible silence at the center of the lost world.
Now the days are sweeter than they used to be,

The memories come more quickly, and the world at twilight,
The world I live in now, is the world I dreamed about
So many years ago, and now I have.
How far it feels from that infatuation with the childish
Dream of passing through a vibrant death into my real life!
How thin time seems, how late the fragrance
Bursting from the captured moments of my childhood
Into the warm evening air that still surrounds me here.
And how the names still throb inside my mind, and how my
    heart dissolves
Into a trembling, luminous confusion of bright tears.

For the texture of this life is like a field of stars

In which the past is hidden in a tracery
Looming high above our lives, a tangle of bright moments

Vibrating like a cloud of fireflies in the warm summer air.
And the glow of each one is a lifetime waning,
Spending itself in the temporary consolations of a mind
Beyond any possibility of happiness, that hovers in the air
A little while and then descends into itself
And the liberation of the clear white sky inside
Where the names float like birds, and all desire dies,
And the life we longed for finds us at the end.

In the Park

This is the life I wanted, and could never see.
For almost twenty years I thought that it was enough:
That real happiness was either unreal, or lost, or endless,
And that remembrance was as close to it as I could ever come.
And I believed that deep in the past, buried in my heart
Beyond the depth of sight, there was a kingdom of peace.
And so I never imagined that when peace would finally come
It would be on a summer evening, a few blocks away from
    home
In a small suburban park, with some children playing aimlessly
In an endless light, and a lake shining in the distance.

Eventually, sometime around the middle of your life,
There's a moment when the first imagination begins to wane.
The future that had always seemed so limitless dissolves,
And the dreams that used to seem so real float up and fade.
The years accumulate; but they start to take on a mild,
Human tone beyond imagination, like the sound the heart
    makes
Pouring into the past its hymns of adoration and regret.
And then gradually the moments quicken into life,
Vibrant with possibility, sovereign, dense, serene;
And then the park is empty and the years are still.

I think the saddest memory is of a certain kind of light,
A kind of twilight, that seemed to permeate the air
For a few years after I'd grown up and gone away from home.
It was limitless and free. And of course I was going to change,
But freedom means that only aspects ever really change,
And that as the past recedes and the future floats away

You turn into what you are. And so I stayed basically the
    same
As what I'd always been, while the blond light in the trees
Became part of my memory, and my voice took on the accents
Of a mind infatuated with the rhetoric of farewell.

And now that disembodied grief has gone away.
It was a flickering, literary kind of sadness,
The suspension of a life between two other lives
Of continual remembrance, between two worlds
In which there's too much solitude, too much disdain.
But the sadness that I felt was real sadness,
And this elation now a real tremor as the deepening
Shadows lengthen upon the lake. This calm is real,
But how much of the real past can it absorb?
How far into the future can this peace extend?

I love the way the light falls over the suburbs
Late on these summer evenings, as the buried minds
Stir in their graves, the hearts swell in the warm earth
And the soul settles from the air into its human home.
This is where the prodigal began, and now his day is ending
In a great dream of contentment, where all night long
The children sleep within tomorrow's peaceful arms
And the past is still, and suddenly we turn around and smile
At the memory of a vast, inchoate dream of happiness,
Now that we know that none of it is ever going to be.

Don't you remember how free the future seemed
When it was all imagination? It was a beautiful park
Where the sky was a page of water, and when we looked up,
There were our own faces, shimmering in the clear air.
And I know that this life is the only real form of happiness,

But sometimes in its midst I can hear the dense, stifled sob
Of the unreal one we might have known, and when that ends
And my eyes are filled with tears, time seems to have stopped
And we are alone in the park where it is almost twenty years
    ago
And the future is still an immense, open dream.

NOTES

"Dorothy Wordsworth": The quoted passages in the third
stanza are from Elizabeth Hardwick's essay on Dorothy
Wordsworth in *Seduction and Betrayal*.

"Each One As She May": The title is that of a story of
Gertrude Stein's in *Three Lives*, and the phrase "for myself
and strangers" in the last line is from *The Making of
Americans*. In line fourteen, the phrase "eternal recompense
and peace" is from Holderlin's poem "To Zimmer," trans.
Michael Hamburger.

"Objects in Autumn": The quoted passages are taken, with a
few changes, from Thomas Reid's *Essays on the Intellectual
Powers of Man*.

"Kinderszenen": The title is that of Robert Schumann's op.
15

"The Echo Chamber": The phrase "moving image of
eternity" in line eleven is from Plato's *Timeaus*, trans.
Benjamin Jowett.

These poems carry dedications:

"A Long Lesson" to John Ashbery
"Objects in Autumn" to Fairfield Porter
"The Echo Chamber" to Darragh Park
"In the Park" to Susan Koethe

Library of Congress Cataloging in Publication Data

Koethe, John, 1945-
    The late Wisconsin spring.

    (Princeton series of contemporary poets)
    I. Title.   II. Series.
PS3561.O35L3   1984   811'.54   84-42574
ISBN 0-691-06620-5 (alk. paper)
ISBN 0-691-01414-0 (pbk.)